Glashütter Verlagswesen

Eine florierende Haus- und Heimindustrie

Glashütte Cottage Industry

a flourishing Supply System

Deutsches
Uhrenmuseum *Glashütte*

Vorwort
Foreword

Bereits am 7. Dezember 1845 wird die Grundlage für das Glashütter Verlagswesen, auch bekannt als die Haus- und Heimindustrie, gelegt. Die Schüler, die ab diesem Tag von Ferdinand Adolph Lange ausgebildet werden, sollen nicht nur Uhrmacher, sondern auch selbstständige Zulieferer werden. Jedem Schüler wird ein Teil der Uhrenherstellung zugewiesen; nach dem Ende der Ausbildung soll er sich dann auf seinem Spezialgebiet selbstständig machen und als Hausindustrieller tätig sein.

Doch um eine präzise Uhr zu bauen, benötigt man nicht nur exakte Einzelteile, sondern auch Werkzeuge und Messinstrumente für die Herstellung. Auch ästhetische Aspekte spielen in den nächsten Jahren eine immer größere Rolle. So wächst die Haus- und Heimindustrie immer weiter; technologische Innovationen werden entwickelt; die Uhrenfabrikation in Glashütte floriert.

Die Stiftung »Deutsches Uhrenmuseum Glashütte – Nicolas G. Hayek« würdigt mit dieser Ausstellung anhand ausgewählter Beispiele die zahlreichen Betriebe, die den Erfolg Glashüttes maßgeblich beeinflusst haben.

The foundation for the Glashütte cottage industry, also known as Glashütte supply system, is laid on December 7, 1845. The students trained on that day by Ferdinand Adolph Lange are destined to become watchmakers and also independent suppliers. Each student is assigned a part of the production of a watch; when his training is completed he can set up shop in his specialty area and become active as a supplier.

To build a precise watch, however, one needs not only precise individual components, but tools and measuring instruments for production as well. Aesthetic aspects also play an increasingly important role in the years to come. Thus the cottage industry continues to grow; technological innovations are developed and the production of watches in Glashütte flourishes.

With this exhibition the Foundation "German Watch Museum Glashütte – Nicolas G. Hayek" pays tribute, using selected examples, to the many different companies that have made a substantial contribution to the success of Glashütte.

Werkzeuge
Tools

Karl Renner – Erste Glashütter Präcisions-Werkzeugfabrik
Karl Renner – First Glashütte Precision Tool Factory

Anzeige Karl Renner & Sohn
Advertisement Karl Renner & Sohn

Präzisions-Schnellbohrmaschine Karl Renner & Sohn
High speed precision drilling machine Karl Renner & Sohn

Voraussetzung für die Uhrmacherei sind spezielle Werkzeuge, Vorrichtungen und Maschinen. Karl Renner (1857–1931) gründet 1894 seine Werkzeugfabrik. Sie produziert Verzahnungs- und kleine Bohrmaschinen, Werkzeuge für die Uhren- und Laufwerkfabrikation sowie vielfältige feinmechanische Teile und Erzeugnisse.

A prerequisite for watchmaking is a range of special tools, devices and machines. Karl Renner (1857–1931) sets up his tool factory in 1894. It produces tooth-cutting and small drilling machines, tools for watch movement production as well as a variety of precision mechanical components and products.

Verzahnungsmaschinen Karl Renner & Sohn
Gearing machines Karl Renner & Sohn

Die »Erste Glashütter Präcisions-Werkzeugfabrik und Werkstätte für Feinmechanik« ermöglicht durch ihre Spezialma-
schinen die Herstellung von Zahnrädern und Trieben in bis dahin ungekannter Präzision. Sie trägt wesentlich zur Blüte
der Glashütter Uhrenproduktion bei. Die Fräs-, Schleif- und Bohrmaschinen, Poliervorrichtungen und Stempeluhren
zeichnen sich durch eine so hohe Qualität aus, dass sie weltweit gefragt sind. Die Firma kann kaum alle eingehenden
Bestellungen bearbeiten. 1945 wird die Firma demontiert.

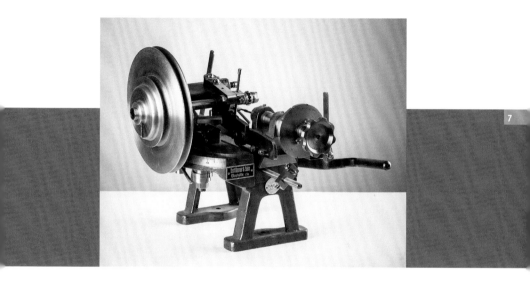

Thanks to its special machines the "First Glashütte Precision Tool Factory and Workshop for Precision Mechanics" makes it possible to produce toothed wheels and pinions with an unprecedented degree of precision.

It makes a significant contribution to the flourishing of watch production in Glashütte. The milling, grinding and drilling machines, polishing devices and time clocks are of such high quality that demand for them is worldwide. The company can hardly keep up with all the orders coming in. In 1945 the company is dismantled.

Otto Lindig – Werkstätte für Feinmechanik Glashütte in Sachsen
Otto Lindig – Workshop for Precision Mechanics Glashütte in Saxony

Aufträge an Otto Lindig, um 1896
Orders to Otto Lindig, around 1896

1855 gründet Otto Lindig (1824–1894) sein Unternehmen. Von Anfang an beliefert er Lange, Assmann, Schneider und Grossmann mit einer Vielzahl von Uhrenteilen, darunter Räder und Triebe.

Mit Unterstützung von Moritz Grossmann beginnt er darüber hinaus mit der Herstellung von Präzisionspendeluhren und Laufwerken. Eine Besonderheit der Firma besteht darin, dass sie Bausätze für Pendeluhren herstellt.

Berechnung der Triebverhältnisse
Calculation of the pinion proportion

In 1855 Otto Lindig (1824–1894) founds his company. From the beginning he supplies Lange, Assmann, Schneider and Grossmann with a large number of watch components, including wheels and pinions. In addition, with the support of Moritz Grossmann, he begins to produce precision pendulum clocks and movements. A particular feature of the company consists in the fact that it produces construction sets for pendulum clocks.

Bestellung der Firma »Girner & Schefuß« bei Otto Lindig, Hamburg 1877
Order of the company "Girner & Schefuß" to Otto Lindig, Hamburg 1877

Nach Otto Lindigs Tod 1894 führt sein Sohn Alfred die Firma zunächst erfolgreich weiter, ehe sie in den Jahren nach dem Ersten Weltkrieg in große wirtschaftliche Schwierigkeiten gerät. 1922 fusioniert sie daher mit der Firma »C. H. Wolf Werkstätte für Präzisions-Mechanik Glashütte in Sachsen« zur Firma »LIWOS«. Dieser Name steht für »Otto Lindig Nachf. C. H. Wolf & Söhne«. Die bisherige Produktpalette der beiden Firmen wird fortgesetzt. Am 1. Juli 1951 wird die Firma in den »VEB Glashütter Uhrenbetriebe« eingegliedert.

Rechnung von Otto Lindig an Max Sanna, München, 1913
Invoice of Otto Lindig to Max Sanna, Munich 1913

Following the death of Otto Lindig in 1894 his son Alfred manages the company successfully until the years following World War I, which bring considerable economic hardship. As a result, in 1922 the company merges with the "Workshop for Precision Mechanics Glashütte in Saxony Carl Heinrich Wolf" to become the firm known as "LIWOS". This stands for "Otto Lindig Nachf. C. H. Wolf & Söhne".The product lines of the two companies are continued. On July 1, 1951, the company is absorbed into the "VEB Glashütter Uhrenbetriebe".

C. H. Wolf – Werkstätte für Präzisions-Mechanik Glashütte in Sachsen
C. H. Wolf – Workshops for Precision Mechanics Glashütte in Saxony

Belegschaft C. H. Wolf, 1910
Staff of C. H. Wolf, 1910

Carl Heinrich Wolf (1844–1925) wagt 1868 nach dreijähriger Lehre und mehrjähriger Tätigkeit bei der Firma »Kunath/ Glashütte« den Sprung in die Selbstständigkeit. Er produziert zunächst, ebenso wie die Firma »Otto Lindig«, Laufwerke für Großuhren und eine Vielzahl von Uhrenteilen, die er an die Glashütter Hersteller liefert. Besonders auf dem Gebiet der Konstruktion von feinmechanischen Werkzeugen offenbart er ein herausragendes Talent. So bietet die Firma auch Schleifapparate für Edelsteine an. 1899 übergibt Carl Heinrich Wolf die Firma an seinen Sohn Georg (1870–1942), der sie weiterführt.

Drehmaschine mit Fußantrieb
Turning lathe with treadle drive

Following three years of training and several years working at the company "Kunath/Glashütte", in 1868 Carl Heinrich Wolf (1844–1925) dares to become independent. At first he produces, like the "Otto Lindig" company, movements for large clocks and a range of watch components, which he supplies to the Glashütte manufacturers. He proves to have exceptional talent, particularly in the area of the construction of precision mechanical tools. As a result the company also supplies grinding devices for precious stones. In 1899 Carl Heinrich Wolf hands the company down to his son Georg (1870–1942), who takes over operational management.

Eingriffszirkel zur Ermittlung und Übertragung von Zahnradabständen
Dephting tool, aid for checking the matching of toothed wheels

»C. H. Wolf« ist die einzige Glashütter Firma, die auch Turmuhren herstellt. Zwei von ihnen, in Possendorf und in Stadt Wehlen, sind noch heute erhalten. Neben ihrer Produktion für die Uhrenindustrie ist das Unternehmen auch außerhalb von Glashütte ein begehrter Zulieferer anderer Industriezweige. Eine Vielzahl technologischer Neuerungen findet ihren Niederschlag in der Produktpalette. So fertigt Carl Heinrich Wolf Zählwerke sowie Telegrafen- und Morseapparate, die überregional begehrt sind. Ein wichtiger Kunde ist beispielsweise die Firma »Siemens & Halske«, Berlin.

Katalog C. H. Wolf, 1919
Catalogue C. H. Wolf, 1919

The company "C. H. Wolf" is the only Glashütte firm that also makes clocks for church towers. Two of these, in Possendorf and in Stadt Wehlen, can still be seen today. Along with its production for the watch industry, the company is a much sought-after supplier to other branches of industry and not only in Glashütte. A number of technological innovations are reflected in the range of its products. The company produces counting devices as well as telegraph and morse code devices, which are much in demand in the region and beyond. One of its important customers is "Siemens & Halske", Berlin.

Ernst Kreissig – Mechanische Werkstätte Glashütte/Sa.
Ernst Kreissig – Mechanical Workshops Glashütte/Sa.

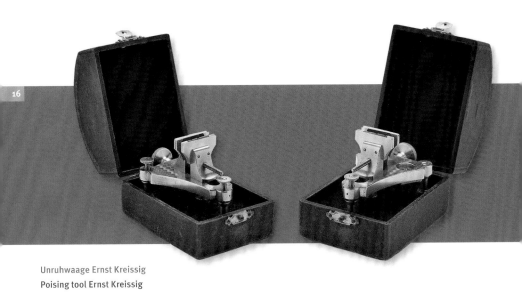

Unruhwaage Ernst Kreissig
Poising tool Ernst Kreissig

Ernst Kreissig (1838–1904) geht zunächst bei Hermann Schneider in die Lehre. Nach dessen Tod übernimmt er 1868 ohne Kapital, aber im Vertrauen auf seine Fähigkeiten, die Werkstatt. Sie konzentriert sich auf die Herstellung von Werkzeugen und Vorrichtungen für die Uhrenfabrikation und Feinmechanik. Ein erster wichtiger Auftraggeber ist dabei die Firma von Moritz Grossmann, die einen Teil ihrer Werkzeugproduktion an Kreissig abtritt. Um das Jahr 1900 beschäftigt die Firma 18 Mitarbeiter. Sie besteht bis 1924.

Ernst Kreissig (1838–1904) begins by undertaking an apprenticeship with Hermann Schneider. Following the latter's death he takes over the workshop; although he has no capital he is convinced of his own capabilities. The company focuses on the production of tools and devices for watchmaking and precision mechanics. One of its most significant initial customers is Moritz Grossmann's company, which cedes a part of its tool production to Kreissig. Around the year 1900 the company employs 18 workers. The company remains operational until 1924.

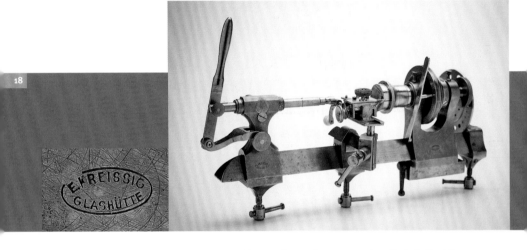

Firmenstempel Ernst Kreissig   Uhrmacherdrehstuhl mit Dreikant-Prismenwange, Ernst Kreissig Glashütte
Company stamp Ernst Kreissig   **Watchmakers swivel chair with triangular lathe bar, Ernst Kreissig Glashütte**

Wichtige Entwicklungen der Firma sind der Glashütter Uhrmacherdrehstuhl mit Dreikant-Prismenwange sowie die Unruhwaage. Auf diesen Gebieten erreicht Kreissig eine bis dahin nicht gekannte Qualität und Präzision, die seine Erzeugnisse auch über Glashütte hinaus begehrt macht. Davon zeugt eine Vielzahl von Auszeichnungen, Ehrenurkunden und Medaillen, unter anderem aus Königsberg, Genf und Wien.
Im Jahr 1900 errichtet Kreissig eine elektrische Zentrale für die Firma. Von ihr werden auch die Deutsche Uhrmacherschule Glashütte und umliegende Gebäude mit Elektrizität versorgt – für die Stadt ein großer Fortschritt.

Auszug Katalog Ernst Kreissig
Extract of the catalogue of Ernst Kreissig

Important products developed by the company include the Glashütte watchmaker's swivel chair with triangular lathe bar and the poising tool. In these fields Kreissig achieves unprecedented quality and precision, which creates a demand for his products from Glashütte and beyond. This is documented by numerous awards, honorary certificates and medals from, among others, Königsberg, Geneva und Vienna.

In the year 1900 Kreissig builds an electrical power plant for the company which supplies electricity to the German School of Watchmaking Glashütte and surrounding buildings – a big step forward for the town.

Messmittel

Dial gauges

Messuhren

GLASHÜTTER
PRÄZISION

R. MÜHLE & SOHN
GLASHÜTTE i. SA.

Robert Mühle – Mechanische Werkstatt
Robert Mühle – Mechanical Workshop

Prospekt Robert Mühle & Sohn
Advertising folder
of Robert Mühle & Sohn

Robert Mühle

Die Familie Mühle zählt zu den alteingesessenen Bewohnern der Region. Der aus Lauenstein stammende George Albert Mühle (1841–1921) gründet 1869 die erste Firma unter dem Namen »Mühle«. Er erlernt zuvor die Konstruktion und Herstellung von Messinstrumenten während seiner Lehrzeit als Mechaniker bei Moritz Grossmann.

Die Firma stellt vorrangig Messinstrumente her, insbesondere Zehntelmaße, Zangenmikrometer, Messuhren und Messtaster. Mit diesen beliefert Mühle die Glashütter Uhrenfirmen sowie andere Industriezweige. Zusätzlich zu seiner eigenen Produktion übernimmt Mühle nach dem Tod Moritz Grossmanns 1885 dessen Werkzeugfertigung.

Wappen der Familie

NEC SPE, NEC METU

Mühle

Familienwappen
Family crest

Urkunde und Ehrenpreis der Stadt Dresden, 1896
Dresden city price and charter, 1896

The Mühle family is among those who have lived in the region for the longest time. George Albert Mühle (1841–1921) from Lauenstein founds the first company under the "Mühle" name. Prior to doing so he learns about the design and manufacture of measurement instruments during his apprenticeship as a mechanic with Moritz Grossmann.

The company produces mainly measurement instruments, in particular dixieme gauges, pincer micrometers, dial gauges and measurement sensors. Mühle supplies these products to Glashütte watch manufacturers and to other branches of industry. In addition to its own products, in 1885 the company takes over the production of tools from Grossmann following the latter's death.

Bildzähler für Filmprojektoren
Frame counters for film projectors

George Albert Mühle nimmt wahrscheinlich den Namen Robert an, nachdem sein Sohn Robert und seine erste Ehefrau früh sterben. Daher trägt auch die Firma den Namen »Robert Mühle«. Aus der zweiten Ehe gehen sieben Kinder hervor. Zwei davon, Max (1874–1944) und Alfred (1878–1940), treten als Mitinhaber ein. Am 1. Juli 1905 wird die Firma in »Robert Mühle & Sohn« umbenannt.

Zu den Produkten der Firma gehören auch ausgefallene Geräte wie Bildzähler für Filmprojektoren oder Mikrometer-Punktmessmaschinen für Schützenvereine. Mit diesen werden Treffer auf der Schießscheibe hundertstelmillimeter-genau vermessen.

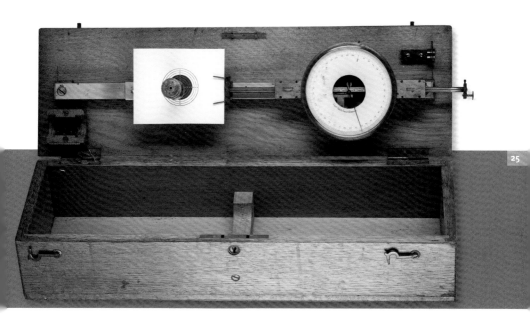

Mikrometer-Punktmessmaschine
Pincer micrometer point measurement machine

George Albert Mühle probably takes on the name Robert after his son Robert and his first wife die at a young age. For this reason the company, too, bears the name "Robert Mühle". His second marriage produces seven children. Two of them, Max (1874–1944) and Alfred (1878–1940), join the firm as co-owners. On July 1, 1905, the company is renamed "Robert Mühle & Sohn".

Among the company's products are also eccentric devices such as frame counters for film projectors or pincer micrometer point measurement machines for shooting associations. The latter are used to measure hits on the target with hundredth of a millimeter precision.

Firmengebäude Robert Mühle
& Sohn, um 1940
**Company building Robert Mühle
& Sohn, around 1940**

Autouhr
Automobile clock

Die aufkommende Verbreitung des Automobils bietet der Firma trotz der Wirtschaftskrise nach dem Ersten Weltkrieg die Chance, neue Produkte auf den Markt zu bringen. Mit Tachometern, Kilometerzählern und Automobiluhren beliefert sie Firmen wie Horch, BMW und Triumph.

Despite the economic difficulties after World War I, the growth in the use of automobiles gives the company an opportunity to take new products to market. The firm supplies customers such as Horch, BMW and Triumph with tachometers, mileage indicators and automobile clocks.

Reklame, um 1925
Advertisement,
around 1925

Im Januar 1920 fusioniert die Firma mit anderen Glashütter Betrieben zur offenen Handelsgesellschaft »Vereinigte Glashütter Rechenmaschinenfabriken, Tachometer- und Feinmechanische Werke A. Burkhardt & Cie. – Saxonia Schumann & Cie. – R. Mühle & Sohn«, kurz »Vereinigte Werke«. Nach Auflösung der »Vereinigten Werke« im Jahr 1929 existiert die Firma »Robert Mühle & Sohn« als einzige wieder eigenständig.

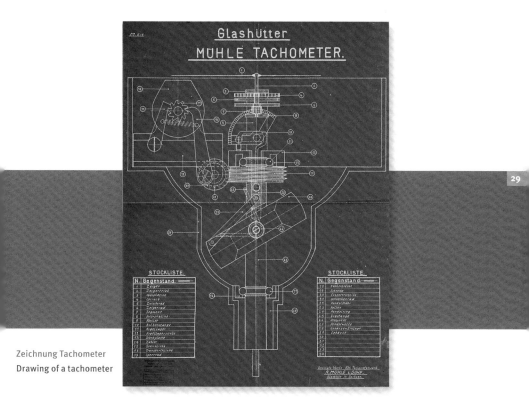

Zeichnung Tachometer
Drawing of a tachometer

In January 1920 the company merges with other Glashütte firms to form the general partnership "United Glashütte Calculator Factories, Tachometer and Precision Mechanical Works A. Burkhardt & Co. – Saxonia Schumann & Co. – R. Mühle & Sohn", abbreviated to "United Works". Following dissolution of the partnership in 1929, the company "Robert Mühle & Sohn" stands once again on its own.

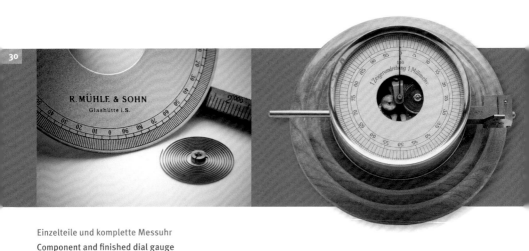

Einzelteile und komplette Messuhr
Component and finished dial gauge

1944 übernehmen die Geschwister Heinz (1910–1993) und Charlotte Mühle (1908–1986), Letztere als stille Teilhaberin, die Firma und führen sie bis zur Demontage und Enteignung 1946 weiter. Der daraus hervorgehende »VEB Messtechnik« wird unter anderem mit der Wartung der Messtechnik der Sowjetischen Militäradministration in Deutschland (SMAD) betraut. 1951 wird die Firma in den »VEB Glashütter Uhrenbetriebe«, kurz GUB, eingegliedert.

abgeliefert am 2.7.1945
1 Kiste enthaltend 17 Marathon-Tachometer MWT1 100

abgeliefert am
1 Kiste enthaltend 100 Ständer Nr. 38
1   "   "   49 Ständer Nr. 38
1   "   "   470 Messuhren Nr. 29 im Etui
1   "   "   121 Messuhren Nr. 29 mit Tol.-Marken im Etui
1   "   "   123 Kleinmessuhren Nr. 31 ohne Etui
1   "   "   162 Messuhren Nr. 29 mit Anlüfthebel im Etui
                    5 Messuhren Nr. 29 mit Anlüfthebel & Tol.-Marken
                                                           im Etui
1   "   "   53 Messuhren Nr. 29 mit Bef.-Öse im Etui
                    6 Messuhren Nr. 29 mit Bef.-Öse (Union-Diehl)
                                                           im Etui
                    9 Messuhren Nr. 29 mit Bef.-Öse & Tol.-Marken
                                                           im Etui
                   26 Messuhren Nr. 29 Fig. 7 in Spez.-Ausführung
                                                     (Gebr.Haake)

1   "   "   143 Messuhren Nr. 33 im Etui
                    3 Messuhren Nr. 33 mit Bef.-Öse,Hebel & Tol.-
                                                     Marken im Etui
1   "   "   40 Messuhren Nr. 33 mit Anlüfthebel im Etui
                   20 Messuhren Nr. 33 mit Hebel & Tol.-Marken
                                                           im Etui
                   19 Messuhren Nr. 33 mit Tol.-Marken im Etui
                   20 Tiefenmessuhren Nr. 35
                    2 Messuhren Nr. 29 Fig. 7 20 mm Messbereich
                                                           im Etui
                    2 Kleinmessuhren Nr. 31 mit Bef.-Öse im Etui
                    1 Kleinmessuhr Nr. 31 mit Bef.-Öse & Tol.-
                                                     Marken im Etui

Auszug Demontagelisten, 1945
Extract of the dismantling lists, 1945

In 1944 the brother and sister Heinz (1910–1993) and Charlotte Mühle (1908–1986), the latter as silent partner, take over management of the firm and direct operations until its dissolution and expropriation in 1946. The company which emerges from this, the state-owned enterprise "VEB Messtechnik" (VEB Measurement Technology) is assigned responsibility for maintenance of measurement technology used by the Soviet military administration in Germany (SMAD). In 1951 the firm is absorbed into the state-owned "VEB Glashütter Uhrenbetriebe" (VEB Glashütte Watch Companies), known as 'GUB'.

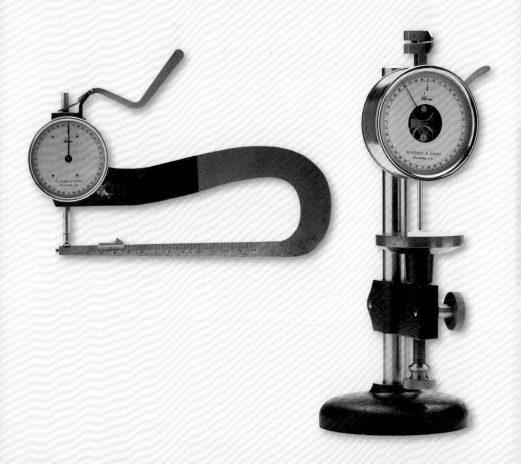

Produktionsraum, um 1950
Production hall, around 1950

Parallel dazu, am 7. Dezember 1945, gründet Hans Mühle (1903–1970) den Familienbetrieb als »Ingenieur
Hans Mühle KG« neu. Ab 1960 hat er seinen Sitz in der Altenberger Straße 35 und produziert Zeigerwerke
für die Manometer der Druck- und Temperaturmessung. 1972 wird der Betrieb als »VEB Feingerätetechnik«
verstaatlicht und 1980 in die GUB integriert.

In parallel Hans Mühle (1903–1970) re-founds the family business on December 7, 1945, under the name
"Ingenieur Hans Mühle KG". From 1960 on it is located in the Altenberger Straße 35 and produces motion works
for manometers used in measuring pressure and temperature. In 1972 the company is nationalised under
the name "VEB Feingerätetechnik" (VEB Precision Instrument Technology) and is integrated into GUB in 1980.

Firmengebäude, 2012
Company building, 2012

1994 gründet Hans-Jürgen Mühle (*1941), der Urenkel von Robert Mühle, den Familienbetrieb ein drittes Mal. Die Firma trägt von nun an den Namen »Mühle-Glashütte GmbH nautische Instrumente und Feinmechanik«.

Produktionsraum, 2012
Production hall, 2012

In 1994 Hans-Jürgen Mühle (*1941), the great grandson of Robert Mühle, starts up the family company for the
third time. From this point on the company bears the name "Mühle-Glashütte GmbH nautische Instrumente
und Feinmechanik"(Mühle-Glashütte Ltd nautical Instruments and Precision Mechanics).

Quarz-Marinechronometer, 1996 ▶
Quartz marine chronometer, 1996

Thilo (l.) und Hans-Jürgen (r.) Mühle
Thilo (l.) and Hans-Jürgen (r.) Mühle

Inzwischen knüpft die Firma in fünfter Generation an die Familientradition an und produziert vorwiegend Armbanduhren sowie Marinechronometer, Schiffsuhren und nautische Instrumente. Seit 2007 wird die Firma von Hans-Jürgen Mühles Sohn Thilo (*1968) geführt.

In the meantime the company, now in its fifth generation, takes up the family tradition and produces primarily wristwatches and marine chronometers. Since 2007 the company is managed by Thilo Mühle (*1968), the son of Hans-Jürgen Mühle.

Stunden u. Minutenzeiger in Stahl u. Gold.

Zu allen Grössen.	Qualität	I.	II.	III.	Gold 14 Kr.
		Mk.	Mk.	Mk.	Mk.
	Birnenform				
	Breguet				
	Lilien				
	Americaform				
	Wadenzeiger				
	do in Gold				
	...astarke				
	Birnenform				

Louis XV. Zeiger 18, 14 u. 8 Kr. Gold gravirt.

1 Dtzd. Paar 18 Kr. 1. Qual.	Mk.	Pf.	1 Dtzd. Paar 14 Kr. II. Qual.	Mk.	Pf.
			1 " " 8 " III. "		

August Gläser – Zeigerfabrik
August Gläser – Watch Hands Factory

◀ Preisliste Zeigerfabrik Gläser
List of prices of hands factory Gläser

Union-Taschenuhr mit Louis XV. Goldzeigern, 1898
Union pocket watch with Louis XV. golden hands, 1898

August Gläser (1833–1886) beginnt im Jahr 1847 seine Ausbildung bei Ferdinand Adolph Lange und gründet kurz darauf seine eigene Manufaktur für die Herstellung von Zeigern. 1878 übernimmt sein Sohn Paul (1860–1930) und später sein Enkel Johannes (1884–1961) die Firma. Sie erlischt 1960.

August Gläser (1833 – 1886) begins his apprenticeship in 1847 with Ferdinand Adolph Lange and shortly thereafter founds his own manufactory for the production of watch hands. In 1878 his son Paul (1860–1930) assumes responsibility for the company, followed by his grandchild Johannes (1884–1961). The company ceases to exist in 1960.

Prägewerkzeug zur Zeigerherstellung
Blanking tool for producing hands

Die aufwendig gearbeiteten und hoch vollendeten Zeiger prägen über lange Zeit hinweg das äußere Erscheinungsbild der Glashütter Uhren. Es werden Zeiger in verschiedensten Größen und Formen angefertigt, in Gold ebenso wie in Stahl – von filigranen, kompliziert gefertigten Louis-XV-Zeigern für Taschenuhren bis zu eher funktional gestalteten Zeigern für Marinechronometer. Eine von den Kunden der Firma immer wieder gelobte Spezialität ist dabei die hohe Qualität der Politur der Zeiger.

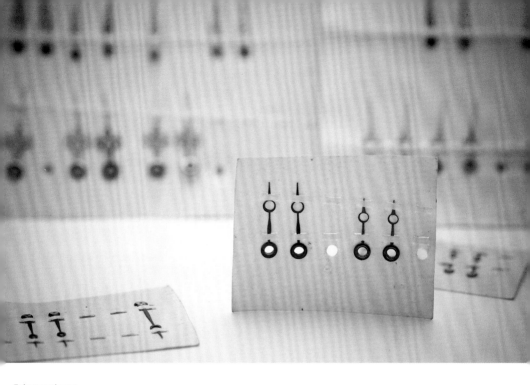

Zeigersortiment
Product line of hands

The elaborately worked and highly finished hands from the manufactory give a distinguished look to watches from Glashütte over an extended period of time. Hands are produced in a great variety of sizes and forms, in gold as well as steel – ranging from filigreed Louis-XV pocket watch hands made using an extremely complicated procedure to more functionally formed hands for marine chronometers. A specialty frequently praised by customers is the high quality of the hands' polish.

Karl Bernhard Kohl – Unruhfertigung
Karl Bernhard Kohl – Balance Manufactory

Unruhschraubenwaage
Balance screw scale

Arbeitsplatz Kompensationsunruhherstellung
Workplace for producing compensation balances

Karl Bernhard Kohl (1832–1908) ist einer der ersten Schüler, die im Jahr 1845 die Lehre beginnen. 1849 gründet er seine eigene Werkstatt. Sein Name ist untrennbar mit der Entwicklung der Glashütter Kompensationsunruh verbunden. Die Erfindung der goldenen Gewichtsschrauben und der geschlitzten Gewindebohrungen im Unruhreif sowie die Entwicklung des Goldankers führen zu einer Präzision, die zu dieser Zeit unerreicht ist. Das in der Ausstellung gezeigte Hämmerwerk zur Verdichtung des Unruhreifs ist ein wesentliches Element zur Sicherung dieser herausragenden Qualität.

Arbeitsschritte der Kompensationsunruhherstellung
Steps for producing compensation balances

Karl Bernhard Kohl (1832–1908) is one of the first students who begin their apprenticeship in 1845. In 1849 he founds his own workshop. His name is inseparably linked with the development of the Glashütte compensation balance. The invention of the gold weight screw and the slit threaded holes in the balance rim as well as the development of the gold pallet fork lead to an unprecedented degree of precision. The hammer mill for compression of the balance wheel, on display in the exhibition, plays an essential role in assuring this exceptional quality.

Richard Grießbach – Unruhfertigung
Richard Grießbach – Balance Manufactory

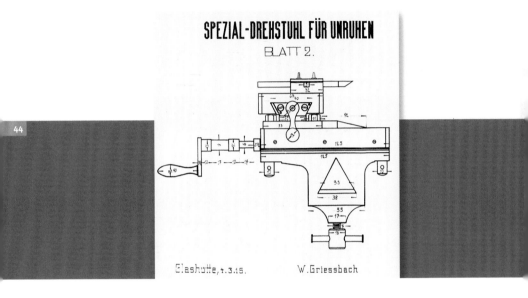

Zeichnung Spezial-Drehstuhl für Unruhen, 1916
Drawing of special lathe bar for balances, 1916

Richard Grießbach (1868–1948) gründet im Jahr 1896, nach mehrjähriger Tätigkeit in der Firma von Karl Bernhard Kohl, seine eigene Fabrik zur Unruhfertigung. Als Spezialität gelten Nickelstahl-Kompensationunruhen für Taschenuhren und Marinechronometer. Durch seine Entwicklungen auf diesem Gebiet verleiht er der deutschen Chronometerfabrikation neue Impulse. Das Markenzeichen »RGG« auf dem Unruhschenkel ist bis heute bei Sammlern Glashütter Uhren begehrt. Sein Sohn Rudolf (1892–1968) führt die Firma bis 1962 weiter. 1992 erfolgt die Reprivatisierung der Firma »Richard Grießbach Feinmechanik GmbH«. Sie produziert in Seyde bei Frauenstein feinmechanische Erzeugnisse und bezieht 2004 ihr neues Produktionsgebäude in Altenberg.

Kompensationsunruh
Compensation balance

After working for many years for Karl Bernhard Kohl, in 1896 Richard Grießbach (1868–1948) founds his own company for the production of balances. His specialty is the production of nickel steel compensation balances for pocket watches and marine chronometers. His developments in this area revitalise German production of chronometers. His "RGG" trade mark on the balance arm remains an item much sought after by collectors of Glashütte timepieces today. His son Rudolf (1892–1968) directs company operations until 1962. In 1992 the re-privatization of the company "Richard Grießbach Mechanical Workshop" followed. A variety of precision mechanical components and products is produced in Seyde. From 2004 on it is located in the new factory in Altenberg.

Carl Ferdinand Goldsche – Gestellteilefertigung
Carl Ferdinand Goldsche – Frame Component Manufactory

Zeichnung Balancier, 1897
Drawing screw press, 1897

Carl Ferdinand Goldsche (1826–1877) zählt wie Karl Bernhard Kohl zur ersten Generation der Lehrlinge, die 1845 bei Lange ihre Ausbildung aufnehmen. Seine Tätigkeit wird beschrieben als: »dreht Pfeiler und setzt die Gestelle zusammen«. Ab 1850 fertigt er in seiner eigenen Werkstatt Platinen und Pfeiler, wesentliche Komponenten der Uhrwerke, mit denen er zunächst Lange und später auch andere Glashütter Uhrenfabrikanten beliefert. Der in der Ausstellung gezeigte Balancier stammt aus den Anfangsjahren der Uhrenfertigung in Glashütte und dient dazu, die einzelnen Teile aus Metallplatten herauszuschneiden.

Balancier
Screw press

Like Karl Bernhard Kohl, Carl Ferdinand Goldsche (1826–1877) belongs to the first generation of apprentices who take up their training in 1845 under Lange. His activity is described as: "turns pillars and assembles frames". From 1850 on he makes plates and pillars in his own workshop, essential components of the movements he supplies initially to Lange and later to other Glashütte watchmakers as well. The screw press on display in the exhibition comes from the early years of watch production in Glashütte and is used to cut out the individual components from metal sheets.

Willy Richter – Edelsteinschleiferei
Willy Richter – Gem Grinding Shop

Arbeitsplatz Steinschleiferei
Workplace for producing gems

Um eine höchstmögliche Präzision zu erreichen, wie sie von Glashütter Uhren verlangt wird, sind eine perfekte Lagerung der Triebe sowie die präzise Fertigung der Ankerpaletten notwendig. Dies wird durch die Bearbeitung entsprechender Edelsteine, vorwiegend Rubine und Saphire, erreicht.
Einer der Spezialisten auf diesem Gebiet ist in Glashütte der Edelsteinschleifer Willy Richter (1896–1967), der seine Werkstatt im Jahr 1921 einrichtet. Neben der Fertigung für die Uhrenherstellung produziert Richter Steine für Messwerkzeuge.

Sortiment Lochsteine
Assortment of jewels

To achieve the highest possible degree of precision that is expected of Glashütte watches, both a perfect positioning of the pinions as well as the precise crafting of the anchor pallets are necessary. This is achieved through the processing of corresponding gems, primarily rubies and sapphires. One of the specialists in this field in Glashütte is the gem grinder Willy Richter (1896–1967), who sets up his workshop in the year 1921. Along with gems used in watchmaking, Richter produces stones for measurement tools.

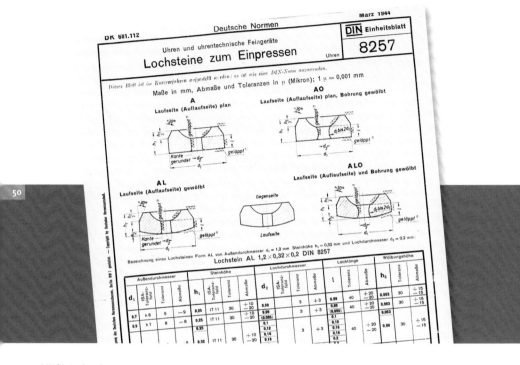

DIN für Lochsteine
DIN standards for jewels

Um 1900 gelingt die synthetische Herstellung von Rubin. Seit 1920 wird er in der Uhrmacherei verwendet. Dieser zeichnet sich gegenüber dem natürlichen Rubin durch eine größere Reinheit und Festigkeit aus. Ein optisches Merkmal für die Präzision der Glashütter Uhren ist die Fassung des zumeist roten Lagersteins in Goldchatons und deren Fixierung mittels gebläuter Schrauben. Nach dem Tod von Willy Richter übernimmt seine Tochter Gisela, verheiratete Gocht (1929 – 2011), das Geschäft und führt es als eigenständiges Unternehmen bis 1991 weiter.

Lochstein in verschraubtem Goldchaton
Jewel in gold chaton

Around 1900 it becomes possible to produce synthetic ruby, and from around 1920 onwards the watch industry uses synthetic ruby exclusively. Compared to natural rubies, synthetic rubies are purer and more stable. An optical marker for the precision of Glashütte watches is the setting of the jewels, usually red, in gold chatons with blued screws. Following the death of Willy Richter his daughter Gisela, married name Gocht (1929–2011), takes over the business and runs it as an independent company until 1991.

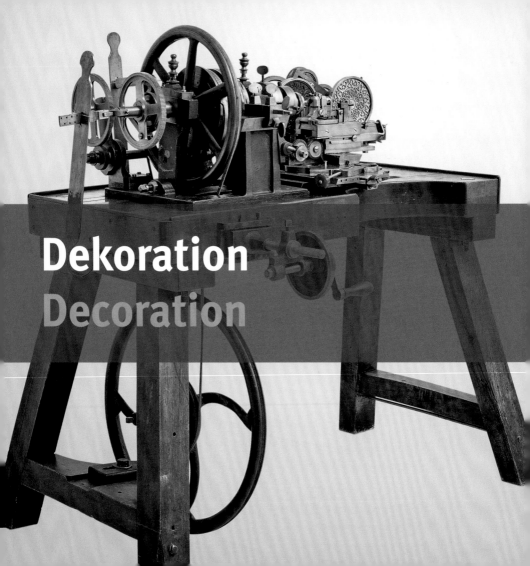

Dekoration
Decoration

Wilhelm Hohnsbein – Guillochieranstalt
Wilhelm Hohnsbein – Guilloches

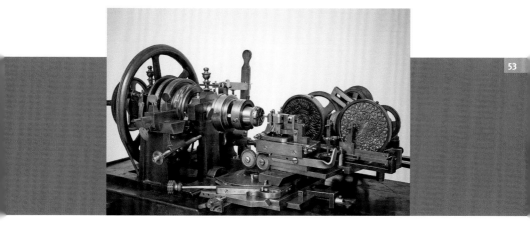

Guillochiermaschine
Guilloche machine

Als Guillochieren bezeichnet man in der Uhrmacherei die Dekoration von Gehäusen, Zifferblättern und Werkteilen mit meist geometrischen Mustern. Dabei werden die Ornamente mit einem Stichel in das Material geritzt. Das Guillochieren wird im Gegensatz zum Gravieren vorwiegend maschinell ausgeführt.

The term guilloche refers in watchmaking to the decoration of cases, dials and movement components with patterns, usually geometric. The ornamental motifs are inscribed into the material using a gouge. In contrast to engraving, guilloche finishings are generally done by machine.

Auftrag und Rechnung für Guillocherarbeiten
Order and invoice for producing guilloches

Wilhelm Hohnsbein (1857–1932) kommt um 1885 nach Glashütte. Zunächst als Mitarbeiter der Firma »A. Lange & Söhne« für die Gehäusefertigung zuständig, macht er sich 1891 mit seiner eigenen Werkstatt selbstständig. Dank seines Wirkens entwickelt sich der Beruf des Guillocheurs als eigenständiger Zweig der Uhrmacherei in Glashütte. Seine Arbeiten weisen eine solche Qualität auf, dass er seine Aufträge nicht nur von den Glashütter Uhrenfirmen, sondern auch aus anderen Regionen erhält. Kurz nach seinem Tod wird die zuletzt von seinem Sohn geführte Firma im Jahr 1934 aufgelöst.

Guillochierte Taschenuhr
Pocket watch with guilloche

Wilhelm Hohnsbein (1857–1932) arrives in Glashütte in 1885. Initially an employee of "A. Lange & Söhne" responsible for the manufacture of watch cases, in 1891 he sets up his own independent workshop. As a result of his activities the profession of "guillocheur" becomes an independent branch of the watchmaking industry in Glashütte. His work is of such high quality that he obtains commissions not only from Glashütte watchmakers but from other regions as well. Not long after his death the company, which is run by his son, is closed in 1934.

Gustav Gessner – Gravieranstalt
Gustav Gessner – Engravers

Auftragsbuch Gustav Gessner, 1884
Order book of Gustav Gessner, 1884

Die Kunst des Gravierens schafft aus den ursprünglich glatten Werkstücken durch Handarbeit ein individuelles Kunstwerk. Das Gehäuse wird mit Ornamenten, Wappen oder Initialen verziert.

Gustav Gessner (1853–1926) erlernt in seiner Heimat Schlesien den Beruf des Graveurs. 1875 gründet er in Glashütte die »Gravieranstalt Gustav Gessner«. Er arbeitet eng mit dem Guillocheur Wilhelm Hohnsbein zusammen. Ihre handwerklichen Fertigkeiten prägen über viele Jahrzehnte das Erscheinungsbild der Glashütter Uhren. Diese werden dadurch zu unverwechselbaren Einzelstücken.

Taschenuhrengehäuse graviert
Engraved case of a pocket watch

The craftsmanship of the engraver turns an originally blank component into an individual work of art.
Cases, cocks and bridges are decorated with ornamental designs, crests or initials.
In his home region of Silesia, Gustav Gessner (1853–1926) learns the engraver's trade. In 1875 in
Glashütte he founds the firm "Gustav Gessner Engravers" and works closely with the guillocheur Wilhelm
Hohnsbein. For many decades their craft skills shape the appearance of Glashütte watches, which thus
become unique works of art.

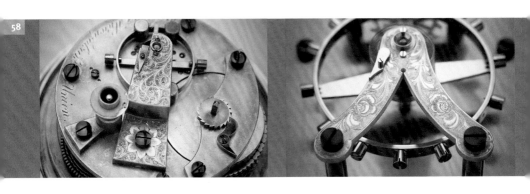

Gravierte Unruhkloben
Engraved balance cock

Eine enge geschäftliche Beziehung und Freundschaft verbindet Gustav Gessner mit Professor Ludwig Strasser, dem langjährigen Direktor der Deutschen Uhrmacherschule Glashütte. Aus dieser Verbindung heraus fertigt Gessner eine Vielzahl von Arbeiten für die Uhrmacherschule. So übernimmt er oftmals die kunstvolle Gravur der Schülerarbeiten, zum Beispiel an Gehäusen und Kloben. Für seine Bemühungen zum Wohle der Stadt wird ihm 1907 das »Ritterkreuz II. Klasse des Albrechtordens« von König Friedrich August III. verliehen. Ab 1926 führt sein Sohn Fritz die Firma bis 1946 weiter.

Graviervorlagen
Engraving models

A close business relationship and friendship binds Gustav Gessner with Professor Ludwig Strasser, the director of the German School of Watchmaking Glashütte for many years. The relationship inspires Gessner to create a great many works for the school. Often he undertakes to enhance the work of students with artful engravings, for example on cases and cocks. In 1907, in recognition of his efforts on behalf of the town, King Friedrich August III awards him the "Knight's Cross II. Class of the Order of Albrecht". From 1926 to 1946 his son Fritz manages the company.